SCOTLAND'S
KINGS & QUEENS

Text by
Chris Tabraham

LOMOND
www.lomondbooks.com

COBVS·5·D·GRATIA

Mary Queen of Scots, Robert the Bruce, Macbeth – these are the names of Scotland's kings and queens that spring immediately to many people's lips. But what of the other 45 kings and queens who sat on the throne of Scotland between its emergence in the 840s and the creation of the United Kingdom in 1707 – the other Mary (yes, there were two), all seven Jameses, four Malcolms, three Alexanders, Constantins, Donalds and Kenneths, two more Roberts, Charleses, Duncans, Davids and Williams, and those whose names stand alone on the royal list: Aedh, Anne, Culen, Dubh, Edgar, Edmund, Edward, Giric, John, Lulach and Margaret? Most have tiptoed quietly out of our collective memory and into the dusty pages of history.

So why does Mary still captivate our hearts over 400 years after her passing? She wasn't the only woman to reign as Queen of Scots, and she wasn't the only sovereign to have their head chopped off – and it has to be said that little of lasting consequence happened during her personal reign, apart that is from the birth of her son, King James VI and I, who united the kingdoms of Scotland and England in 1603.

King Robert the Bruce's reign, on the other hand, was of momentous significance for Scots, then and today, for his great victory over the English at Bannockburn in 1314 secured the nation's continuing sovereignty and independence at a time when all seemed doomed.

Then there is poor King Macbeth, one of Scotland's great kings, whom we remember for all the wrong reasons, and none of the right ones, the eleventh-century monarch forever damned by the pen of a seventeenth-century English playwright called Shakespeare. Yet just about the only thing Macbeth did wrong was fail to get himself a good 'spin doctor'!

The story of Mary, Robert the Bruce, Macbeth and the others is told in this book. Each in their own way has a unique contribution to make. Together they combine to tell the story of a nation forged in the furnace of the Dark Ages over a thousand years ago, and joined with England in 1707 to form the United Kingdom of Great Britain and Ireland.

PORTRAIT OF A KING JACOBUS 3 D GRATIA REX SCOTORUM (James III by the Grace of God King of Scots). An artist, as yet unidentified, was commissioned by King James VI in the late sixteenth century to paint portraits of the first five Jameses. Though none of the portraits was painted from life, there is evidence to suggest they were based on earlier, contemporary work. The artist describes each monarch as rex Scotorum, 'King of Scots'; unlike kings and queens of England, Scottish sovereigns were deemed rulers of their people, not of the land.

A WARRIOR SOCIETY
The 'Battle Stone' at Aberlemno kirkyard, near Dunnichen, Angus, depicts the crushing defeat of King Egfrith of Northumbria by King Bridei and his Picts at the Battle of Nechtansmere in 685. In 843, the crowns of Pictland and Scotland were united under Kenneth I.

Shortly before AD 800, the first Viking longships appeared off Scotland's west coast, lured there by the rich treasures in monasteries such as Iona. The Scottish kings, themselves invaders from Ireland several centuries earlier, moved eastward for their security, to the land of the Picts, Scotland's oldest inhabitants. Less than fifty years later, Kenneth mac Alpin ('son of Alpin'), king of the Scots, had overthrown the king of the Picts and created a new 'united kingdom'. King Kenneth I called his new country Alba (the Gaelic word formerly applied to the whole of the island of Britain). We know it better as Scotland.

The country over which Kenneth I ruled was much smaller than present-day Scotland, reaching from the great rivers of Clyde and Forth in the south to the chilly waters of the Moray Firth and the snow-capped mountains of the north. To the north lay the Vikings, by now rulers of Orkney, Shetland and the Western Isles and fast encroaching on mainland Scotland too; to the south lay the ancient British kingdom of Strathclyde and the more recently established Anglo-Saxon kingdom of Northumbria.

Kenneth I did not directly succeed his father, Alpin, as king of the Scots. Given the pitfalls inherent in such a warrior society, there was no sense having as heir a young lad untried in combat. What was needed was someone strong and battle-hardened, and closely related by blood, to continue the dynasty. During the entire 200-year period of the MacAlpin dynasty, not one son directly succeeded his father; most were cousins, one or two brothers or nephews. Another rarity was for a king to die peacefully in his bed, for most were killed in battle, or murdered by kinsmen. One king, Constantin II, Kenneth mac Alpin's grandson, clearly

The MacAlpin Dynasty

Kenneth I	(c.843-59) - nicknamed 'mac Alpin'; died Forteviot; buried Iona; succeeded by his brother
Donald I	(859-63) - killed near Scone; buried ?; succeeded by his nephew
Constantin I	(863-77) - killed in Angus fighting the Vikings; buried Iona; succeeded by his brother
Aedh	(877-78) - killed in Strathallan by Giric; buried Aberdeenshire?; succeeded by his cousin
Giric	(878-89) - died at Dundurn, Perthshire; succeeded by his nephew
Donald II	(889-900) - killed at Forres fighting the Vikings; buried Iona; succeeded by his cousin
Constantin II	(900-42) - abdicated and became a monk; died 952 in St Andrews and buried there; succeeded by his cousin
Malcolm I	(942-54) - killed in the Mearns fighting the men of Moray; buried Iona; succeeded by his cousin
Indulf	(954-62) - killed near Banff fighting the Vikings; buried ?; succeeded by his cousin
Dubh	(962-67) - nicknamed 'the Black'; killed near Forres by Culen; buried ?; succeeded by his cousin
Culen	(967-71) - nicknamed 'the Whelp'; killed in Lothian by King Riderch of Strathclyde; buried ?; succeeded by his cousin
Kenneth II	(971-95) - killed at Fettercairn, Angus; buried Iona; succeeded by his cousin
Constantin III	(995-97) - killed in ?; buried ?; succeeded by his cousin
Kenneth III	(997-1005) - killed at Monzievaird, Angus, fighting Malcolm II; buried ?; succeeded by his cousin
Malcolm II	(1005-34) - killed at Glamis, Angus; buried Iona; succeeded by his grandson
Duncan I	(1034-40) - nicknamed 'the Gracious'; killed in Moray by Macbeth; buried Iona; succeeded by his cousin
Macbeth	(1040-57) - killed at Lumphanan, Aberdeenshire, by Malcolm III; buried Iona; succeeded by his stepson
Lulach	(1057-58) - nicknamed 'the Simple'; crowned Scone; killed Essie, Aberdeenshire, by Malcolm III; buried Iona; succeeded by a distant cousin, Malcolm, founder of the Canmore dynasty.

A VIKING KING

The 'king' from the Lewis chess-set, discovered in 1831. The quite extraordinary chess pieces were made by someone somewhere in the Viking world, perhaps Trondheim, in Norway, around 1100, and their find-spot in the Outer Hebrides serves to highlight the plain fact that in the Middle Ages much of northern and western Scotland was under the sway of the kings of Norway, and not Scotland.

KING KENNETH I
Kenneth mac Alpin ('son of Alpin') united the crowns of Scotland and Pictland around 843. The unknown artist of this sixteenth-century portrait, from the Seton Armorial, depicts the founder of the Scottish kingdom in heroic pose, trampling on the vanquished Picts.

could not stand the pace, abdicating his throne in 942 for the tranquillity of the monastery cloister.

The first MacAlpin kings set about consolidating the dynasty's hold over their new kingdom. Then, around 900, they turned their minds to expansion, casting their covetous eyes chiefly over the lands to the south, to Strathclyde and Northumbria, both increasingly ravaged by the Danes. It wasn't long before Strathclyde and Lothian were effectively under Scottish domination.

Such was their confidence that they began also to strike deep into Anglo-Saxon England. In 937 King Constantin II confronted King Athelstan in battle at Brunanburgh. It was the first of many battles to be fought between the 'auld enemies'. The Scots lost on that occasion, but when the two armies met again, at Carham on the River Tweed in 1018, King Malcolm II's Scots claimed the victory. As a result, Scotland's border moved south to its present line.

But as the Scots advanced south, they left their northern border exposed. Around 900 the Vikings, having already grasped Orkney and Shetland, sailed south across the Pentland Firth and seized Caithness and Sutherland also. The northern Picts, left to defend themselves, grew ever more resentful of their southern kinsmen and rebelled. They finally achieved mastery of the Scottish throne in 1040 when their thane, Macbeth, slew his cousin, King Duncan I, in battle near Elgin, and seized the throne. For

KENNETH I
'First in line'

Kenneth mac Alpin was born around AD 800 just as the Vikings began striking terror in the hearts of his people, the Scots. By 840 he was their king, and turning his gaze upon the throne of Pictland.

The story goes that around 843 he invited the feuding Pictish warlords to feast with him at Scone, where he had them treacherously killed. Kenneth I, whom later genealogies claimed was descended from the legendary Fergus Mór 'the great', founder of the Scottish kingdom of Dál Riáta (modern Argyll), was destined to establish a royal dynasty that continues to rule to this day.

MACBETH
'Hero or villain?'

Macbeth reigned for 17 years, a remarkable achievement given the doubt surrounding his royal credentials. Later chroniclers blackened his name, telling of a 'tyrannous regime' and of 'a loyal people refusing to submit any longer to a man of no higher rank than themselves'. Shakespeare, in his 'Scottish play', simply echoed these sentiments.

Yet this was not necessarily how Macbeth's contemporaries saw him. He was 'the generous king' who brought prosperity, whose hold on power was secure enough for him to undertake a lengthy pilgrimage to Rome, and who at his death was laid to rest on Iona alongside his valiant predecessors. How apt his name then – MacBeathadh, 'son of life'. This was no rebellious upstart but a sovereign confidently enthroned. That he was eventually undone at Dunsinnan cannot deny Macbeth his rightful place in history, as Scotland's last great Celtic king.

KING MACBETH
Macbeth, newly enthroned as King of Scots, plots the downfall of Banquo and his son Fleance. George Cattermole captures Macbeth on canvas just as we imagine him to have been - dark and devious. In reality, Macbeth was no murdering upstart but a prince of the royal blood, who reigned for 17 years - no mean achievement in those turbulent times.

DUNADD,
CRADLE OF KINGS
The Dark-Age hillfort of Dunadd, dominating Moine Mhor, or 'Great Moss', in Argyll's Kilmartin Glen, was a royal residence of the early Scottish kings of Dál Riata until the Vikings increasingly threatened their existence after 800. With Kenneth I's creation of the new kingdom of Scotland around 843, Dunadd was forsaken for new royal seats in the east, including Dunfermline.

IONA,
GRAVEYARD OF KINGS
From the time of Aedán mac Gabhrain's inauguration as King of the Scots of Dál Riata at Iona in 574, the holy island of St Columba was held in the highest regard by Scotland's kings, and became the royal mausoleum. Only after the Hebrides were ceded to the king of Norway in 1098 was Iona abandoned and replaced as royal mausoleum by Dunfermline.

the next seventeen years, King Macbeth reigned over his people, commanding their respect and sufficiently confident of his hold on power to undertake a lengthy pilgrimage to Rome, the only Scottish sovereign to do so. But Macbeth's defeat at Dunsinnan Hill, Perthshire, in 1054, at the hands of Duncan's son, Malcolm, led ultimately to his downfall. His stepson and successor, King Lulach, reigned for a mere seven months before Malcolm finally grasped the throne for himself.

Lulach's name is hardly ever heard today, yet he is the first king on record to be crowned on the Moot Hill at Scone, the ancient king-making centre beside the River Tay just to the north of Perth. Lulach was also the last king to be buried on Iona, the royal mausoleum of the MacAlpin dynasty. With the accession in 1058 of King Malcolm III, the Scottish kings and queens turned their backs on their ancestral homeland in the west and looked increasingly southward to England for fame and glory.

IONA
'Graveyard of kings'

In 574, so it is written, an angel appeared to St Columba commanding him to ordain Áedán mac Gabhráin king of the Scots of Dál Riata. This is among the earliest references in Europe to the inauguration ceremony of a king. Columba's Iona subsequently became the favoured place of burial of the early Scottish kings.

The Reilig Odhráin ('Oran's graveyard'), beside the later medieval abbey on Iona, was subsequently appropriated by the great clan chiefs of the region, including the MacDonalds and MacLeods, and thereafter by the ordinary folk of the district. It is still in use today. Alas, no stone there can now be assigned to any particular king, but no one can doubt the testimony of the documents, and the simple fact that the bones of the early kings of Scots, from Kenneth mac Alpin to Lulach, lie on that hallowed isle.

The Jolly Beggars, anonymous painting. *According to Sir Walter Scott, '"The Jolly Beggars", for humorous description and nice discrimination of character, is inferior to no poem of the same length in the whole range of English poetry'. Despite his mastery of monologue this cantata was the closest Burns came to drama. He contemplated dramatising the folk-tale of Omeron Cameron and there were plans for a play entitled 'Rob McQuechan's Elshon', but neither materialised.*

Barely had King Malcolm III – his nickname Canmore means 'big chief' – settled on his throne than England was thrown into turmoil by the Norman Conquest. Scotland now found itself confronting Vikings to north and south, for William the Conqueror's ancestor, Rollo, founder of the Duchy of Normandy, had been a Viking pirate. To make matters worse, Malcolm allowed Edgar, the last male representative of the Anglo-Saxon House of Wessex, to take shelter in Scotland. He even married Edgar's sister, Margaret. William the Conqueror responded by invading Scotland, penetrating as far as the Tay before having to return south to quell continuing unrest in his new land. Little did Malcolm realise, as he pledged allegiance to William that day at Abernethy, that therein was sown the seed-corn that would give future kings of England to understand they were overlords of Scotland also.

King Malcolm and his eldest son, Edward, died side by side fighting the Normans. Queen Margaret, heart broken, passed away just four days later. Those nobles who resented the growing foreign influence at court seized their chance and, in a palace coup, levered Malcolm's brother, Donald Ban, onto the throne. For the next four years, Donald III vied with Malcolm's sons for supremacy before finally being deposed by Edgar, the third son, in 1097.

SYMBOLS OF SOVEREIGN POWER
'Crowns and stones'

King Edgar (1097-1107) is the first Scottish sovereign depicted wearing a crown, and yet we cannot properly talk of Scottish coronations until 1331. For centuries, placing a new sovereign on the Stone of Destiny had been central to the king-making ceremony. By 1200, however, Scots were attaching greater importance to the Christian rites of coronation and anointment as practised on the Continent. Yet despite repeated pleas to Rome, permission was always refused on the specious grounds that the kings of Scots were vassals of the kings of England, and needed their permission. Naturally the English refused.

The breakthrough came in 1329, shortly after Robert Bruce's death. The Papal Bull issued by Pope John XXII was final recognition by Christendom's highest authority of the independence of the Scottish Crown. David II was duly anointed and crowned at Scone two years later.

The Canmore Dynasty

Malcolm III	(1058-93) - nicknamed 'Canmore' ('big chief'); born ? (c1031); crowned Scone; killed at Alnwick, Northumberland, fighting the Normans; buried Tynemouth (body later reburied in Dunfermline Abbey); succeeded by his brother
Donald III	(1093-4) - nicknamed 'Donald Ban'; born ? (c.1033); crowned ?; deposed; succeeded by his nephew
Duncan II	(1094) - born ? (c.1060); crowned ?; killed Kincardineshire; buried Dunfermline Abbey; succeeded by the uncle he had deposed
Donald III	(1094-7) - deposed for a second time; died 1099 in a Forfarshire prison; succeeded by another nephew
Edgar	(1097-1107) - born ? (c.1072); crowned ?; died Edinburgh Castle; buried Dunfermline Abbey; succeeded by his brother
Alexander I	(1107-24) - nicknamed 'the Fierce'; born ? (1077/8); crowned ?; died Stirling Castle; buried Dunfermline Abbey; succeeded by his brother
David I	(1124-53) - nicknamed 'the Saint'; born Dunfermline Palace (c.1080); crowned ?; died Carlisle Castle; buried Dunfermline Abbey; succeeded by his grandson
Malcolm IV	(1153-65) - nicknamed 'the Maiden'; born ? (1141/2); crowned Scone; died Jedburgh Castle; buried Dunfermline Abbey; succeeded by his brother
William I	(1165-1214) - nicknamed 'the Lion'; born ? (1142/3); crowned Scone; died Stirling Castle; buried Arbroath Abbey which he had founded; succeeded by his son
Alexander II	(1214-49) - born Haddington (1198); crowned Scone; died Kerrera, Argyll; buried Melrose Abbey; succeeded by his son
Alexander III	(1249-86) - nicknamed 'the Glorious'; born Roxburgh Castle (1241); crowned Scone; died Kinghorn, Fife, following a fall from his horse; buried Dunfermline Abbey; succeeded by his granddaughter
Margaret	(1286-90) - nicknamed 'the Maid of Norway'; born Tonsberg Castle, Norway (1283); died at sea off the Orkneys on her way to Scotland; buried Bergen, Norway; no obvious successor.

MALCOLM CANMORE, FOUNDER OF A DYNASTY

Malcolm III was more popularly known as Canmore (from the Gaelic ceann mór, 'big chief'). Although Malcolm defeated King Macbeth at Dunsinnan, north-east of Scone, in 1054, he had to wait another four years before removing both Macbeth and his successor, Lulach, from the scene and ascending the throne himself.

KING DAVID 'THE SAINT'
David I (pictured left with his grandson, Malcolm IV) depicted posthumously on a charter granting lands and other rights to the monks of Kelso Abbey, Roxburghshire. David of Scotland was the first British sovereign to invite the 'reformed' Benedictine orders to settle in the British Isles, and in the wake of the Tironensians of Kelso followed the Augustinians, Cistercians, Premonstratensians,

DAVID I
'Sair saint for the crown'

Scottish society in the Middle Ages was intensely God-fearing and everyone therefore gave to the Church. But no one gave more than King David I. It was later said of David that he was 'a sair (sore) saint for the croun' because he almost exhausted the royal coffers founding so many monasteries – over 20 in all, including those at Holyrood, Melrose and Dunfermline, where he was laid to rest. David was a devout Christian, just like his mother, St Margaret. When he died his people mourned their loss. Abbot Ailred of Rievaulx, a personal friend, wrote: 'I know that priests and clerics grieve; nuns and monks whom he embraced as brothers grieve; knights grieve, whose friend rather than lord he knew himself to be; the widows whom he protected grieve, as do the orphans whom he comforted, the poor whom he supported, the wretched whom he cherished.'

What Donald Ban's supporters feared most now manifested itself openly. Within a year of his enthronement, Edgar had formally ceded the Viking-held lands in the west to the kings of Norway, so abandoning the homeland of his ancestors. Iona was forsaken as the royal mausoleum and replaced by the monastery at Dunfermline, close by the River Forth, where his father and mother had wed in 1069. Furthermore, had Edgar not died unmarried and childless, he would undoubtedly have been succeeded by his son, for the ancient Celtic system of tanistry, whereby the crown was passed around various branches of the royal family, was now passed over in favour of the European model of succession by primogeniture (first-born).

These continental influences gained their maximum force in the twelfth century with the reforming programmes of Malcolm and Margaret's youngest son, King David I, and his two grandsons who succeeded him, King Malcolm IV and King William I (David's only son, Henry, had died shortly before his father). Together these three kings, whose combined reigns spanned more than a century, comprehensively transformed Scotland from a Celtic state to one more fully in the European mainstream. They also reorganised the Church from top to bottom and introduced new reformed Benedictine orders such as the Cistercians and Augustinians. They also established towns (burghs) for the promotion of trade and exports, and introduced the minting of silver coinage.

'WE THREE KINGS' King Alexander III of Scotland sits on King Edward I of England's right hand, and Prince Llewelyn ap Gruffydd of Gwynnedd, on Edward's left, at a gathering of the English Parliament c 1270. Their respective royal arms are shown above their heads. Alexander and Edward were brothers-in-law, whilst Llewelyn and Robert the Bruce's first wife, Isabella, were distant cousins.

But most importantly of all, they encouraged foreigners to settle in Scotland. Many surnames we today regard as being as Scottish as 'haggis and neeps' are in fact foreign – they include Wallace ('le Walys', an incomer from Wales), Bruce (from Brux in Normandy) and, of course, Stewart (formerly hereditary stewards of the bishops of Dol in Brittany).

By the time William I died in 1214, Scotland had almost been transformed out of all recognition; so too its royal family. Son now succeeded father, as naturally as night followed day, parliament regularly met under the sovereign's watchful gaze, and statutes replaced swords as the chief instruments of justice.

Almost, but not quite. These were still unsettled times, and the kings of Scotland did not have their troubles to seek, from disgruntled nobles, from rebellious provinces such as Moray and Galloway, as well as from beyond their realm, most critically England. David I actually died in England, at his new castle of Carlisle in 1153, following his acquisition of Cumbria and Northumbria from the English Crown. His grandson William's experience of England, though, was very different, for he was held prisoner there, at Richmond Castle, Yorkshire, for several months in 1174; on his release he thanked God and St Thomas of Canterbury by founding Arbroath Abbey.

But by the time the thirteenth century dawned, Scotland and England had largely come to a peaceful accommodation, leaving the confident Canmore dynasty to look once again at reclaiming their lost lands. The death in battle of the mighty

ROYAL MAUSOLEUM
The imposing abbey church of Dunfermline Abbey has a special place in the history of Scotland, as the royal mausoleum of the Canmore dynasty. On this site, the great warrior-king Malcolm III married his saintly queen, Margaret, around the year 1170, and the loving couple were subsequently laid to rest there. The present great Benedictine abbey was built over their tombs by their youngest son, King David I, who was also buried here, as was King Robert the Bruce. King Charles I was one of several royal heirs born in the adjacent royal palace, in 1600, but his headless corpse lies buried in far-off Westminster Abbey.

warrior Somerled, 'King of the Isles', at Renfrew in 1164, was the prelude for a renewed 'push', and by 1200, William I had taken back Caithness and Sutherland in the north, and the islands of Bute and Arran in the west. Further gains followed, and the flow stemmed only briefly with King Alexander II's death on campaign near Oban in 1249. His son, Alexander III, earned his nickname 'the Glorious', when in 1266 he put his seal to the Treaty of Perth, by which King Magnus IV of Norway relinquished sovereignty. Scotland was now bigger than it had ever been; it even included the Isle of Man, which it subsequently lost to England.

The thirteenth century for Scotland was a 'Golden Age', and not just because of peace with England, and the return of old territories, but economically also. And when Alexander III remarried in 1285, aged 45, there was every prospect that his young French queen, Yolande, would produce a son and heir. Alas, four months later Alexander lay dead below a cliff in Fife, following a fall from his horse. His crown passed to his three-year-old granddaughter, Margaret, daughter of the King of Norway.

The Scots now prepared to have a female as their sovereign, the first country in feudal Europe to do so. But when Margaret too died tragically four years later while on her voyage to Scotland to be crowned, the curtain fell on the Canmore dynasty and the Scots, without either king or queen, were thrown into utter confusion.

ROYAL QUEENS

In 1286, Princess Margaret, daughter of the king of Norway, succeeded her grandfather, Alexander III, as sovereign of Scotland. She was just three years old. Alas, the little queen died in 1290 before she could be formally crowned. Nevertheless, she has the distinction of being the first queen regnant in western Europe.

Over two centuries passed before the Scots acclaimed their second queen, Mary Queen of Scots. She was barely a week old when she ascended the throne, but although she outlived her ancestor by many years she too had a tragic life, and a tragic end, on the executioner's block at Fotheringhay Castle, England, in 1587.

Mary's namesake, Mary II, who ruled jointly with her husband, William II, 200 years later, never once visited her Scottish subjects. Neither did her younger sister, Queen Anne, who in 1707 presided over the Act of Union that created the United Kingdom of Great Britain.

EUROPE'S FIRST QUEEN *Margaret Queen of Scots, depicted here on a nineteenth-century stained-glass window in Lerwick Town Hall, Shetland, was western Europe's first queen regnant. Alexander III's granddaughter is better known to history as 'the Maid of Norway' because her father was King Eric II of Norway and she was just three years old when she inherited the throne of Scotland in 1286. Alas, the little queen never did see the country over which she nominally ruled for four years; she fell gravely ill on the voyage from Bergen and breathed her last in the Bishop's Palace, in Kirkwall, in 1290.*

BERWICK-UPON-TWEED – BORDER TOWN
The date Friday 30 March 1296 will be forever etched on the memories of the people of Berwick-upon-Tweed. The townsfolk of Scotland's chief burgh and port had just finished celebrating Easter when suddenly a 30,000-strong English army, with King Edward I at their head, stormed the town walls and ran amok through the streets. By Low Sunday two-thirds of the town's population – 7,500 men, women and children – lay dead or dying. That brutal act heralded the bloody and prolonged Wars of Independence.

The Balliol and Bruce Dynasties

First interregnum (1290-92) - Edward I of England supervises the 'Great Cause', to see who should succeed Margaret 'the Maid of Norway' to the throne. Edward chooses

John (1292-96) - surname Balliol, but nicknamed 'Toom Tabard' ('empty surcoat'); born Barnard Castle, Co. Durham, England (c.1245); crowned Scone; exiled to France; died Bailleul-en-Vimeau, Picardy (1313/14); buried Normandy; replaced by

Second interregnum (1296-1306) - Edward I of England attempts conquest of Scotland through the Wars of Independence. Interregnum ends with enthronement of

Robert I (1306-29) - nicknamed 'the Bruce'; born Turnberry Castle, Ayrshire (1274); crowned Scone; died Cardross, Dunbartonshire; buried Dunfermline Abbey (body) and Melrose Abbey (heart); succeeded by his son

David II (1329-1371) - born Dunfermline Palace (1324); crowned Scone (1331); died Edinburgh Castle; buried Holyrood Abbey; succeeded by his nephew, Robert Stewart, founder of the Stewart dynasty.

(Edward Balliol, son of King John (see above), briefly claimed the throne and was crowned king at Scone 1332; after much toing and froing he was eventually deposed in 1336; died Yorkshire 1365 (?).)

No sooner had Queen Margaret's body been returned to Norway for burial than the rival contenders began to advance their claims to her throne; before that year was out there were thirteen of them! Most were rank outsiders, but two were joint-favourites – John Balliol, Lord of Galloway, and Robert Bruce, Lord of Annandale (not the King Robert but his grandfather).

There was very little between the two claimants; both were descended from David, grandson of David I and younger brother of Malcolm IV and William the Lion. John Balliol was descended from David's elder daughter, Margaret, and Robert Bruce from her younger sister, Isabella, making John's the more senior line. However, Robert was nearer in descent – just one stage removed, not two like John. Over the course of 1291-2 the 'court', gathered in Berwick Castle under Edward I of England's watchful gaze (as the late King Alexander's brother-in-law, the Scots had no reason to question his credentials as presiding judge), considered the matter of the succession. It gave its judgement in November 1292: John Balliol. Two weeks later, St Andrew's Day (30 November), John was crowned king at Scone.

King John was doomed from the very start. Suspicions were soon aroused as to Edward of England's real intentions, and when he began to interfere directly in the running of John's realm – for example, summoning John regularly to report on Scottish matters, and demanding Scottish military and financial help in his fight against France – the Scots' patience snapped. In 1295 they effectively 'sidelined' their sovereign and signed a mutual assistance pact, the 'auld alliance', with the French. Edward was furious. The king who had spent most of his adult life fighting – in civil wars at home, on Crusade, against the Welsh – wasn't going to let the Scots off so easily.

And so he invaded. In March 1296 he crossed the River Tweed and let his army run amok through the streets of Berwick, Scotland's main town and port. In April he inflicted inglorious defeat on the Scottish host at Dunbar, and in June at Montrose he stripped King John of his crown, sceptre and sword. By August, he was heading back to London with John as his prisoner and the Stone of Destiny as his prize. Although he had chosen not to be crowned king at Scone, he was confident he had conquered Scotland. He hadn't. He had merely sparked off the Wars of Independence, a bloody struggle that would last on and off for over fifty years, in which the Scots fought to regain their sovereignty.

The fightback started almost immediately, even though Scotland was without a sovereign. The lead was taken

'TOOM TABARD'
The doomed John Balliol with symbolic broken crown, sceptre and sword, and torn tabard, or surcoat – a reference to his humiliation in Montrose 1296 when Edward of England had King John's symbols of sovereignty stripped from him and his tabard ripped to shreds (whence his nickname 'Toom Tabard', 'empty surcoat').

THE BRUCE

The equestrian statue of King Robert the Bruce overlooks the battlefield of Bannockburn where, in 1314, the great king sent 'proud Edward's army homeward tae think again'. The Scottish victory over the English at Bannockburn did not bring an end to the Wars of Independence with England, but what it did achieve was the unqualified support by the Scots for Bruce as their sovereign king, after years of bitter internecine rivalry with the Balliols.

not by Robert Bruce 'the Competitor' (he had died in 1295), nor by his son, also Robert, (who with extensive lands in England as well as Scotland, had too much to lose) but by William Wallace, who exacted revenge for Berwick and Dunbar at the Battle of Stirling Bridge in 1297. Other Scots risked all by joining the resistance. Only when Robert Bruce (II) died in 1304 did his son, also Robert, emerge from the shadows and join the fight for independence. In March 1306 he was crowned King Robert I at a hastily arranged ceremony at Scone. The Bruce dynasty had come.

King Robert's luck was in almost from the start. In 1307 his arch-enemy, Edward I 'Hammer of the Scots', died beside the Solway sands preparing yet again to invade. His successor, Edward II, had none of his father's military skills, and Bruce was soon seizing castles and evicting English garrisons. He was also soon taking the offensive, carrying the fight into England. Finally, in 1314, at the great Battle of Bannockburn, Bruce led his Scots to resounding victory over the 'auld enemy', effectively freeing his country from English domination. When fifteen years later he passed peacefully away at his manor of Cardross, beside the Clyde, Scotland was once again sovereign and free.

David II, Bruce's son, was just five when his father died. The weakness was immediately exploited by those bearing a grudge against the Bruces, chiefly Balliol supporters who had been stripped of their lands and inheritance. Led by the late King John's son, Edward, they landed in Scotland in 1332, defeated the Scottish army near Perth and 'crowned' Edward king at Scone. The other King Edward, Edward III, grandson of the 'Hammer of the Scots' and every bit as bellicose, was minded to assist. Thankfully though, as far as the Scots were concerned, Edward III had his eye on another throne, and in 1337 he invaded France, so heralding the Hundred Years' War.

SCOTLAND VERSUS ENGLAND
'Auld enemies'

In 937 Constantin II, grandson of Kenneth mac Alpin, first king of Scots, confronted Athelstan, grandson of Alfred the Great, first king of England, on the battlefield. They weren't to know it, but the opening shot in that encounter was to herald a bitter struggle between the two countries that would last for 700 years.

There have been many bloody encounters between the 'auld enemies', among them Carham, 1018 (Scottish victory), Stirling Bridge, 1297 (Scottish victory), Bannockburn, 1314 (Scottish victory), Flodden, 1513 (English victory) and Pinkie, 1547 (English victory). Many a wife was widowed and many a child orphaned down the centuries. But ever since James VI of Scotland crossed the Border in 1603 to become James I of England also, the two warring nations have managed, by and large, to settle their differences peacefully. Today, the Scottish thistle and the English rose intertwine with each other in a way unimagined by our ancestors – on the sports field.

GARRISON CASTLES
During the Wars of Independence, royal castles such as Edinburgh Castle (pictured here) were seized by King Edward of England and used as garrison castles for his troops. The Scots tried their utmost to recapture them. One dark night in March 1314, shortly before Bannockburn, Bruce's nephew, Sir Thomas Randolph, with a hand-picked assault party, made the perilous ascent up the northern precipice, caught the English garrison off guard and retook the fortress.

'AULD ENEMIES'
King David II pictured (left) shaking hands with his brother-in-law King Edward III of England around 1350, when David was a prisoner of Edward's in the Tower of London. By now, Edward had come to realise there was no glory to be got in Scotland and had his eye on a far bigger prize – France. In 1356, shortly after the English victory at Poitiers, and the capture of King Philip of France, David was returned to Scotland. The bloody and prolonged Wars of Independence were at an end.

BANNOCKBURN 1314
'Fight for freedom'

On Midsummer's Day 1314, on boggy ground to the south of mighty Stirling Castle, the greatest battle in Scotland's history was fought.

Bannockburn was a real 'David and Goliath' struggle, with some 8000 Scots up against 17,000 seasoned English troops. Robert Bruce may well not have done battle at all had he not slain in single combat the young nephew of the Earl of Hereford, Sir Henry de Bohun, in a skirmish the previous evening. Emboldened by the act, Bruce resolved to abandon his guerrilla tactics and confront the 'auld enemy' head on.

As the sun rose on the following morning, Bruce ordered his infantry to attack. Soon the English, ineptly positioned on the boggy ground, were trapped between the Bannock Burn and the River Forth. Many were drowned, others were cut down by their pursuers or by their own comrades desperate to escape the carnage. So full of English dead was the Bannock Burn that it was said the Scots could cross without getting their feet wet. Bannockburn was undoubtedly Bruce's finest hour.

With little commitment from Edward of England, the war in Scotland fizzled out – now more of a civil war than a struggle for independence. When David II was captured near Durham by the English in 1346, it was he who was doing the invading, not Edward III!

David II spent eleven years as a prisoner in the Tower of London. When he was eventually returned, his ransom terms were so exorbitant – 100,000 merks payable over ten years – that he very soon found it impossible to keep up with the instalments. The two kings even discussed, and agreed, a possible 'union of the crowns', should David die childless, but the Scottish parliament refused to ratify it.

Despite all these constitutional and financial concerns, David contrived to bring economic stability and good governance back to his realm during what remained of his reign. When he died at Edinburgh Castle in 1371, aged only 47 and childless, he handed over to his nephew and successor, Robert, 7th High Steward of Scotland, a country confident and secure.

THRONE OF SCOTLAND

In the Crown Room in Edinburgh Castle, on display beside the Honours of Scotland, the nation's Crown Jewels, lies the Stone of Destiny, sometimes known as the Stone of Scone. This humble piece of Perthshire sandstone is a powerful icon of Scottish nationhood, a tangible symbol linking the present generation of Scots back through the centuries to their distant forebears, the Picts.

STONE OF DESTINY
'Throne of Scotland'

From time immemorial the Stone of Destiny at Scone was where the kings of Pictland were inaugurated. When Kenneth I united Scotland and Pictland around 843, that tradition continued. The Moot Hill ('meeting hill') became known as the hill 'of melodious shields', referring to the clashing of shields at the acclamation ceremony.

But then came Edward I of England in 1296. He forcibly removed the Stone of Destiny to Westminster Abbey, England, where he had it enclosed within a golden chair, the Coronation Chair. From that time on the ancient stone was used to enthrone the kings and queens of England, and from 1714 the kings and queens of Great Britain also.

On 30 November (St Andrew's Day) 1996 the Stone of Destiny was formally returned to Scotland. Now it rests in the Crown Room in Edinburgh Castle, alongside those other symbols of national sovereignty, the Honours of Scotland. The Stone will only ever leave Scotland again when there is a coronation in Westminster Abbey.

THE SECOND KING JAMES
King James II was just six when he ascended the throne. He was also 'James of the Fiery Face' because of a large birthmark, a feature which this portrait, painted posthumously, carefully ignores. James hadn't only a fiery face, he had a fiery temper too, and during his reign he showed it frequently. He brought down the over-mighty House of Black Douglas, and removed the last remaining English garrison from Scottish soil, at Roxburgh Castle. Tragically, he died there - killed by one of his own cherished siege guns.

THE FIRST KING JAMES
When James I became king at the age of 12, he was a prisoner of King Henry IV of England, having been captured by English pirates off the Firth of Forth. When he returned home, aged 30, he had a new determination to reassert the authority of the Royal Stewarts. This portrait, by an unknown artist, depicts the first King James as a sovereign confident and assured.

The Stewarts reigned for 343 years, by far the longest of any dynasty. When the seventh of their line, King James V, uttered the immortal words: 'It cam wi' a lass, it will end wi' a lass' on his deathbed in Falkland Palace in 1542, he implied that the dynasty would end with his daughter, Mary, then barely a week old. He was proved partly wrong, for although the dynasty did end with a lass, she turned out to be not his daughter Mary but his great-great-great granddaughter Anne.

But who was the lass who began the dynasty? Her name was Marjorie, the daughter of King Robert the Bruce. She had wed Walter, the 6th High Steward of Scotland, in 1315, the year after Bannockburn, and baby Robert was born just a year later. It would be another 55 years before he was crowned King Robert II, the first of the Stewart dynasty.

The problem with the first Stewart was exactly the opposite of the last Bruce; he had too many children, not too few – 22 in all, though only four were strictly legitimate. With so many offspring demanding titles and lands, poor, gentle, ageing 'King Bob', as Dr Johnson described him, found it increasingly difficult to cope. He retired to the comparative peace of his native Ayrshire, leaving his squabbling sons to contest the Stewart inheritance.

Robert II's successor was his first-born, John. Just about the only sensible thing he did was to style himself King Robert III on his accession in 1390, the name John being considered too unlucky, what with its Balliol connotations. By then a kick from a horse had added to his problems, and for the rest of his 16-year reign, the reins of government were held by his younger brother, Robert, Duke of Albany. The two siblings could not have been more

The Stewart Dynasty

Robert II (1371-90) - 7th High Steward of Scotland; born Paisley (1316); crowned Scone; died Dundonald Castle, Ayrshire; buried Scone; succeeded by his son

Robert III (1390-1406) - born Paisley (c.1340); crowned Scone; died Dundonald Castle; buried Paisley Abbey; succeeded by his son

James I (1406-37) - born Dunfermline Palace (1394); crowned Scone (1424); killed (murdered) Perth by noblemen; buried Perth; succeeded by his son

James II (1437-60) - born Holyrood Palace (1430); crowned Holyrood Abbey (1437); killed accidentally Roxburgh; buried Holyrood Abbey; succeeded by his son

James III (1460-88) - born (?) Stirling Castle (1452); crowned Kelso Abbey; killed near Sauchieburn, Stirlingshire, by noblemen; buried Cambuskenneth Abbey; succeeded by his son

James IV (1488-1513) - born ? (1473); crowned Scone; killed Flodden, Northumberland fighting the English; buried Sheen Abbey, Surrey; succeeded by his son

James V (1513-42) - born Linlithgow Palace (1512); crowned Stirling Castle; died Falkland Palace, Fife; buried Holyrood Abbey; succeeded by his daughter

Mary I (1542-67) - born Linlithgow Palace (1542); crowned Stirling Castle; abdicated Lochleven Castle, Kinross (1567); executed Fotheringhay Castle, England (1587); succeeded by her son

James VI (1567-1625) - born Edinburgh Castle (1566); crowned Church of the Holy Rude, Stirling; becomes also King James I of England and Ireland (1603) and creates 'Great Britain'; died Theobalds Park, Hertfordshire, England; buried Westminster Abbey; succeeded by his son

Charles I (1625-49) - born Dunfermline Palace (1600); crowned Holyrood Abbey (1633); executed Whitehall Palace, London; buried Windsor Castle; succeeded by his son

Charles II (1649-85) - born St James's Palace, London (1630); crowned Scone (1651); died Whitehall Palace, London; buried Westminster Abbey; succeeded by his brother

James VII (1685-89) - born St James's Palace, London (1633); not crowned; deposed (1689); died Chateau de St Germain-en-Laye, France (1701); buried Paris; succeeded jointly by his daughter and son-in-law

Mary II (1689-94) - born St James's Palace, London (1662); not crowned; died Kensington Palace, London; buried Westminster Abbey. Ruled jointly with

William III (1689-1702) - born Binnenhof Palace, The Hague, Holland (1650); not crowned; died at Kensington Palace, London, following a fall from his horse; buried Westminster Abbey. Succeeded by his sister-in-law

Anne (1702-14) - born St James's Palace, London (1663); not crowned; formally adopted royal style Queen of Great Britain, France and Scotland (1707); died Kensington Palace, London, the last Stewart sovereign; buried Westminster Abbey; succeeded by her third cousin, Prince George, Elector of Hanover, founder of the Hanoverian dynasty.

THE ROYAL 'LOGO' The royal arms of King James V include almost all the icons of Scottish sovereignty and nationhood - the Lion Rampant (adopted by William I 'the Lion'); two Unicorn supporters, gorged with simple coronets and chained (first used by James I); the crest with the Lion Crowned and holding the Sword and Saltire, surmounted by the royal motto IN DEFENS ('In Defence'); and the national emblem, the Thistle, at the base. The one icon absent from this 'achievement' is the Sceptre. This omission was put right after James V had the Sceptre remade to its present appearance in 1536; it replaced the Saltire in the crested Lion's left paw.

A PLACE TO RELAX
The impressive palace of Linlithgow (above) was a welcome stopping-place for the royal family along the busy road between Edinburgh and Stirling. The Stewart queens especially liked its tranquillity and fresh air, and both King James V (1512) and Mary Queen of Scots (1542) were born there.

FROM ABBEY TO PALACE
When in Edinburgh, the Stewarts much preferred the more amenable royal guesthouse at Holyrood Abbey (right) to the 'richt windy and unwholesome' Edinburgh Castle. When in 1566 Mary Queen of Scots gave birth to Prince James, she did so at the castle, but solely for reasons of security and not comfort.

ROYAL PALACES
'At home with the royals'

Sovereigns need to be seen by their subjects. Television makes that task much easier today, but in medieval times the royal family had no choice but to travel constantly around their realm.

Royal palaces were everywhere, from Ayr to Inverness. And where there were none, they stayed in abbey guesthouses. The guesthouse at Dunfermline Abbey, the royal mausoleum, served as an unofficial royal residence for both the Canmore and Bruce dynasties.

Under the Stewarts, the castles at Edinburgh and Stirling emerged as principal centres of the royal court, with the palaces at Linlithgow and Falkland serving as 'retreats', where they could relax away from the public gaze. By 1500, Edinburgh had become the chief town of the realm, and the sovereigns thereafter based their principal residence there. However, they chose not to live up on the windy castle rock, but amid the fading grandeur of Holyrood Abbey. The Palace of Holyroodhouse is there yet, the British monarchy's one official residence in Scotland.

A SPORTS CENTRE
The Royal Stewarts, male and female, were fond of sport and leisure, and one of their favourite 'sports centres' was Falkland Palace, depicted here around 1640. The Falkland estate was seized by James II from the Earl of Atholl, executed for his part in James I's murder. Thereafter, it was used by every sovereign for hunting, hawking and other leisure activities. The 'real tennis' court built there for James V in 1539 is the only one to survive, the others at Holyrood and Linlithgow having long gone.

different, Robert III introverted and inadequate (he wrote for his own epitaph 'Here lies the worst of kings and the most wretched of men'), Albany resourceful yet compassionate. By all accounts he would have made a good king. He certainly seems to have done his best to become one, closely implicated in the death (or was it murder?) of Robert III's first-born, David, Duke of Rothesay, at Falkland Palace in 1402, as well as the capture by the English of the next-in-line, James, in 1406. But Albany never quite made it to the throne, and has gone down in history as Scotland's 'uncrowned king'.

The fates of the first five King Jameses make for sorry reading. James I was murdered in 1436 by his nobles who found him cowering in a Perth sewer; James II was killed at the siege of Roxburgh in 1460 when one of his own guns exploded; James III was stabbed to death in a humble cottage near Stirling in 1488 following humiliating defeat at the hands of his nobles at the Battle of Sauchieburn; James IV was hacked to pieces by the English on the battlefield of Flodden, Northumberland, in 1513; and James V died 'a broken reed of a man' at Falkland in 1542 after another English defeat, this time at Solway Moss.

But this catalogue of woes masks real achievements by the Stewarts. These included the re-establishment of firm royal authority by the first two Jameses, including bringing down the mighty House of Black Douglas, the repossession of Orkney and Shetland from the king of Norway, the establishment of Edinburgh as the nation's capital, by James III, the overthrow of the treacherous

CROWN JEWELS
'The honours of Scotland'

The Honours of Scotland are the nation's Crown Jewels. The Crown, Sceptre and Sword are the oldest royal regalia in the United Kingdom and among the oldest surviving in Christendom. They were created in Scotland and Italy during the reigns of James IV and James V, and were first used together as coronation regalia at the enthronement of the infant Mary Queen of Scots in Stirling Castle on 9 September 1543. They were last used at Charles II's coronation as King of Scots, at Scone on 1 January 1651.

That these priceless jewels survive at all is a miracle. They have been buried not once but twice in their 500-year-long existence – the first occasion in the 1650s to hide them from Oliver Cromwell, the second as recently as World War II, to prevent them falling into enemy hands.

Today they are proudly on display in the Crown Room in the royal castle of Edinburgh, alongside another symbol of Scottish sovereignty, the Stone of Destiny.

ROYAL REGALIA

On 4 February 1818, the Scottish Officers of State gathered on the stair outside the Crown Room in Edinburgh Castle. Standing beside them was an anxious Walter Scott, whose pleas to the Prince Regent (the future George IV) had resulted in a Royal Warrant permitting him to search for the Honours of Scotland, locked away in 1707 following the Treaty of Union with England. The group watched in silence as the masonry blocking the doorway was removed. In the darkness beyond they spied a great iron-bound oak chest. They approached with great apprehension, for there was the suspicion that the chest was empty. Scott later wrote:

'The chest seemed to return a hollow and empty sound to the strokes of the hammer, and even those whose expectations had been most sanguine felt at the moment the probability of disappointment. The joy was therefore extreme when, the ponderous lid of the chest being forced open, the Regalia were discovered lying at the bottom covered with linen cloths, exactly as they had been left in 1707. The reliques were passed from hand to hand, and greeted with the affectionate reverence which emblems so venerable, restored to public view after the slumber of more than a hundred years, were so peculiarly calculated to excite.'

KING AND QUEEN
King James V (pictured left) married his second queen, Marie (pictured right), daughter of the Count of Guise, in 1540. James's first queen, Madeleine, daughter of King Francois I of France, had died in 1537 shortly after coming to Scotland. Both marriages strengthened the 'auld alliance' between the two countries, but led directly to James's untimely death in 1542, aged 30, following the defeat of the Scots by the English at Solway Moss. Queen Marie thereafter ruled as Queen Regent, determined to stem the rising tide of Protestantism. She failed, and died in Edinburgh Castle in 1560, within a year of the passing of the Act of Reformation.

A RENAISSANCE PALACE
Stirling Castle was perhaps James V's favourite royal palace. His father, James IV, had lavished huge sums on it, including most memorably the majestic great hall (recently restored). James V's principal contribution was a new palace (seen here to the right of the Prince's Tower), for his and Queen Marie's use. Sadly, James never saw it finished, for he died at Falkland Palace just as the workmen were beginning to pack up their tools.

MacDonalds, Lords of the Isles, by James IV, and the creation of some of Europe's finest Renaissance architecture, including the royal palaces at Falkland and Stirling, by James V.

James V died at Falkland just six days after the birth of his daughter Mary at another royal palace, Linlithgow. Mary became only the second female to inherit the throne. She lived just 44 years – but what a life! Thirteen were spent in hiding in France, nineteen as

a prisoner in England, and only twelve in the land of her birth (and for one of those she was a prisoner too). She was queen in two countries – France and Scotland – and would have been queen in a third – England – also. She was three times married: to the French Dauphin, to the debauched Lord Darnley and the dastardly Bothwell; and three times widowed. She never saw her father, she miscarried of twins, was separated from her son shortly after his birth in 1566, never to see him again, and almost died twice in accidents – once in a fire in Stirling Castle and the second time following a hazardous ride over the bleak Border landscape for a tryst with her lover Bothwell.

In the end, Mary met a similar fate to the first five Jameses; that is, she died unnaturally, executed at Fotheringhay Castle, England, in 1587 on the orders of her cousin, Queen Elizabeth of England. Mary adopted as her motto 'En ma fin est mon commencement' – 'In my end is my beginning'. Why she chose it remains a mystery, like so much of her life, but it has proved the perfect epithet. Her significance may not have been so profound when she was alive, but since her parting she has become one of the towering figures of Scottish history. In the hour of her departing began the legend that has become 'Mary Queen of Scots'.

There was one lasting achievement of Mary's reign. In 1566 she gave birth to a son, Charles James, in Edinburgh Castle (the name Charles was quietly dropped because of its Catholic associations). When, in 1567, Mary was compelled to abdicate her throne, the little boy was proclaimed King James VI. Thirty-six years later, upon the death of his aunt, Queen Elizabeth, James became king of England also. Within days of hearing the news, James was progressing around his new country proclaiming the new 'Great Britain'. For the remaining period of the Stewart dynasty, the kings and queens of Scotland were also the kings and queens of England, and the histories of the two great nations become inextricably intertwined.

The Union of the Crowns in 1603 was emphatically not a union of the two nations. But the later Stewarts, from King James VI down to Queen

SCOTLAND'S TRAGIC QUEEN

Mary Queen of Scots reigned in person for just six years of her 44 years on this earth. On 24 July 1567, whilst a prisoner on Lochleven Island, near Kinross, she was compelled to abdicate in favour of her son, James VI. A year later she contrived to escape her watery prison only to end up spending the rest of her tragic life a prisoner of her cousin, Queen Elizabeth of England.

TRIPLE CROWNS
James VI of Scotland's coronation as James I of England was the fulfilment of a dream. Another step had been taken along the road to Union with England. James preferred to be called Rex Britanniae Magnae et Franciae et Hiberniae, 'King of Great Britain and France and Ireland'. 'Great Britain' was his own invention, part of his grand plan for the union of Scotland and England. The reference to France was pure nostalgia, nothing more, for the English Crown had long surrendered all claim to that land.

Anne, showed increasingly scant regard for their northern kingdom. James returned just once, in 1617 as part of his Golden Jubilee celebrations, despite promises he would visit regularly. His son, King Charles I, even though a Scot himself (he was born at Dunfermline Palace in 1600), was equally con-temptuous; he was quick enough to be crowned king of England on his accession in 1625, but eight more years would pass before he could be bothered to come north for his Scottish coronation held in Edinburgh.

By then Charles had already shown further contempt for his fellow Scots by attempting to foist Anglicanism on them rather than their preferred Presbyterianism. It wasn't long before ruler and ruled were at loggerheads and there was civil war. The unrest quickly spread to England and Ireland, and in the end the king who believed he had the 'divine right' to rule, lost his head, literally, in 1649.

The Scots might have profoundly disagreed with King Charles, but they also profoundly disagreed with the English parliament's decision to execute him. They moved quickly to dismiss Oliver Cromwell's offer of a 'united commonwealth of England and Scotland' and declared their support for their late sovereign's son, Charles, by crowning him Charles II, King of Scots, at Scone on 1 January 1651 (he

UNION OF THE CROWNS
'The thistle and the rose'

On 8 August 1503 James IV wed Margaret Tudor, daughter of Henry VII of England, in the Gothic splendour of the abbey church of Holyrood, a union celebrated as 'the marriage of the Thistle and the Rose' after the respective emblems of the two royal dynasties. That marriage subsequently proved to be of momentous importance for both countries.

Exactly a century later, following the death of his aunt Queen Elizabeth of England, James VI of Scotland, the grandson of James IV and Margaret, journeyed south to London for his coronation as James I of England in Westminster Abbey. One of the greatest ironies in British history was about to unfold: after centuries of English monarchs attempting to wrest the throne of Scotland, it was a Scot who would seat himself on the throne of England.

was not crowned King of England until 1660).

Charles II's coronation was the last at Scone, indeed the last in Scotland. He never returned to Scotland, even though he reigned as its king for another 35 years. His brother, King James VII (and II of England), only ever visited Scotland in his capacity as Duke of Albany, not as king, and the last three Stewarts – Mary II, William II and Anne – never visited at all and so were never crowned sovereigns of Scotland. In the event, Charles II's coronation visit of 1651 was the last by a reigning sovereign until King George IV made his triumphant tour in 1822, 171 years later!

In 1707 the seemingly inevitable happened – Scotland and England were formally joined in political as well as regal union. When Queen Anne, the last of the Stewarts, gave her consent to the Act of Union, she consigned the kings and queens of Scotland, and the kings and queens of England also, to the dusty pages of history. From henceforth they would be kings and queens of the United Kingdom of Great Britain and Ireland.

QUEEN ANNE
'Last of the line'

The last of the Stewart dynasty was Queen Anne; as James V had predicted in 1542, the line would 'gang [go] wi' a lass'. Anne had succeeded her brother-in-law, William II, as sovereign of both Scotland and England in 1702. When in 1707 Scotland and England joined together to create the United Kingdom of Great Britain and Ireland, the long line of kings and queens in both countries came to an end. Thereafter they would be kings and queens of Great Britain.

ACT OF UNION

Queen Anne receives a copy of the Treaty of Union from her Scottish Commissioners; Sir Walter Monnington's painting at Westminster records the very moment in 1707 when Scotland and England finally settled their differences and joined in political as well as regal union. There would be no more kings and queens of Scotland and England - henceforth they would be sovereigns of the new kingdom of Great Britain.

Kings and Queens of Scotland

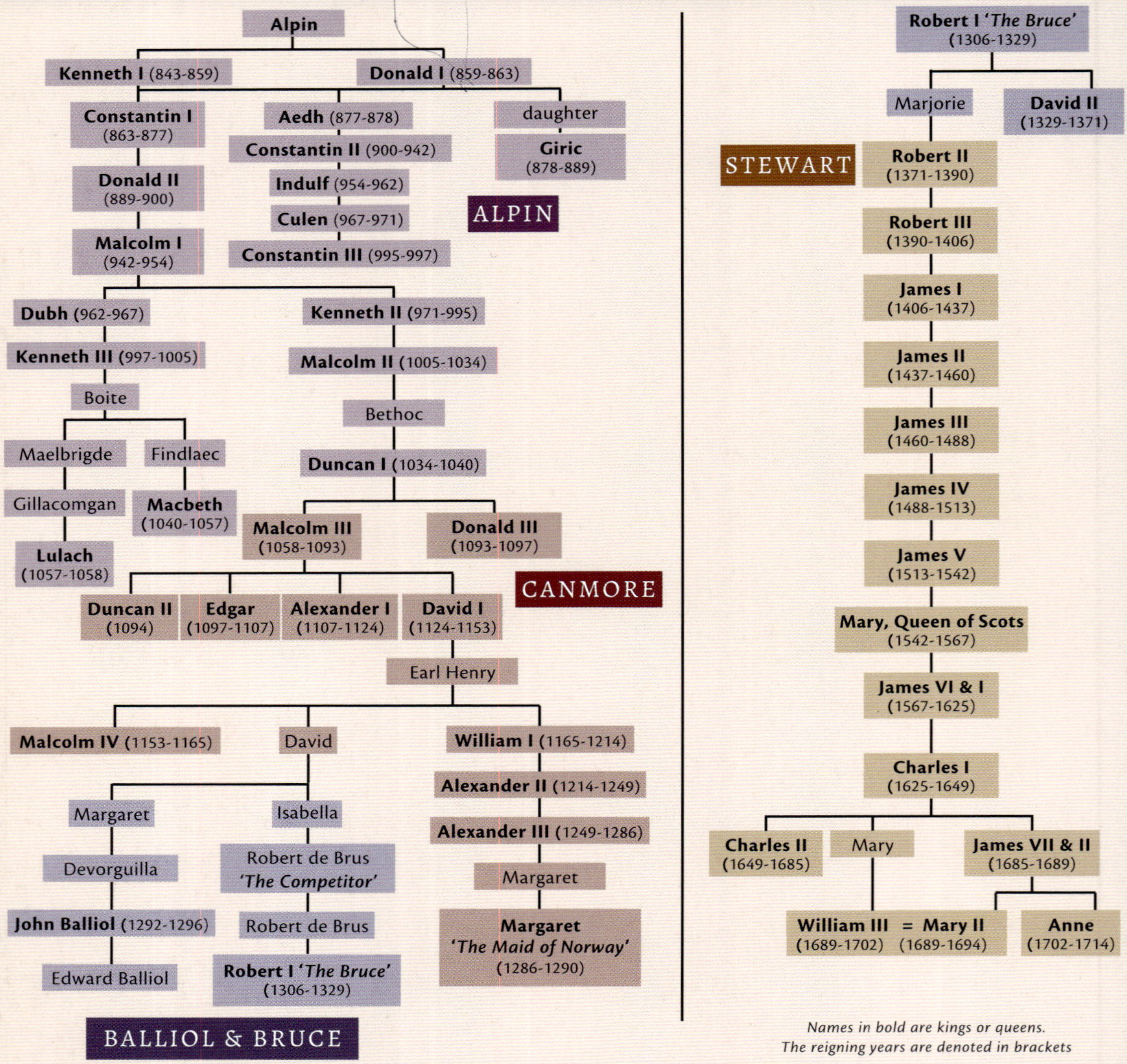

Names in bold are kings or queens.
The reigning years are denoted in brackets

Published by Lomond Books, 13-14 Freskyn Place, East Mains Industrial Estate,
Broxburn EH52 5NF
This edition 2018.
First published in Great Britain in 2004

Text by Chris Tabraham

Photographs © 2018 by:
Colin Baxter: Pages 4,8,9,10,14,16,18,19,24,25,28
Bridgeman Art Library: page 7
By kind permission His Grace the Duke of Roxburghe: page 12
By permission of the British Library: page 20
Court of the Lord Lyon: page 17
Crown Copyright: Reproduced courtesy of Historic Scotland: pages 1,15,21,23,27
Crown Copyright: Palace of Westminster Collection page 31
Glasgow Museums: Art Gallery & Museum, Kelvingrove page 29
National Museum of Scotland: page 5
National Trust for Scotland: page 26
Scottish National Portrait Gallery: pages 2, 22 top & bottom, 28 top left & top right, 30
The Royal Collection ©2003, Her Majesty Queen Elizabeth II: page 13
Trustees of the National Library of Scotland: pages 6,11

A CIP Catalogue record for this book is available from the British Library.

ISBN 9781842046616
Printed in Singapore

Front Cover Photographs clockwise from left to right:
Mary Queen of Scots © Glasgow Museums:
Art Gallery & Museum Kelvingrove
Crown © Crown Copyright: Reproduced by courtesy of Historic Scotland
Robert the Bruce statue © Colin Baxter
King James VI & I © Scottish National Portrait Gallery
Edinburgh Castle © Colin Baxter
Lion Rampant Flag © Trustees of the National Library of Scotland
Back cover photograph Stirling Castle © Colin Baxter

LOMOND
www.lomondbooks.com